A rusty nail is sticking out of the dogs' kennel.

One day Kevin is running

back to the kennel very fast.

He slips. Oh no! He skids all the way past the nail.

The nail cuts a long gash in him. He cries in pain. 'Ow, ow!'

Wellington runs to help Kevin. He is bleeding from the long gash.

Kevin has to go to see the vet. He has a pill to stop the pain.

The vet puts stitches in Kevin to mend the long gash.

Kevin has to stay with the vet until he is well again.